Contents

What is a volcano?

A volcano is a mountain. But it is different from most mountains. A volcano can suddenly send **gases**, **ash**, and hot, melted rock into the air. A volcano can **erupt**!

Some **eruptions** look like bright fireworks. Other eruptions shoot gray smoke into the air.

There are volcanoes all over the world. Let's take a look!

Red-hot fact!
The word "volcano" comes from the name Vulcan. Vulcan was the Roman god of fire.

KINGFISHER READERS

level 3

Volcanoes

Claire Llewellyn and Thea Feldman

KINGFISHER
NEW YORK

KINGFISHER
LONDON & NEW YORK

Copyright © Macmillan Publishers International Ltd 2012
Published in the United States by Kingfisher,
175 Fifth Ave., New York, NY 10010
Kingfisher is an imprint of Macmillan Children's Books, London.
All rights reserved.

Distributed in the U.S. and Canada by Macmillan,
175 Fifth Ave., New York, NY 10010

Library of Congress Cataloging-in-Publication data
has been applied for.

Series editor: Thea Feldman
Literacy consultant: Ellie Costa, Bank St. College, New York

ISBN: 978-0-7534-6762-6 (HB)
ISBN: 978-0-7534-6763-3 (PB)

Kingfisher books are available for special promotions
and premiums. For details contact: Special Markets
Department, Macmillan, 175 Fifth Ave., New York, NY 10010.

For more information, please visit
www.kingfisherbooks.com

Printed in China
9 8 7 6
6TR/0116/WKT/UNTD/105MA

Picture credits
The Publisher would like to thank the following for permission to reproduce their material. Every care has
been taken to trace copyright holders.
Top = t; Bottom = b; Center = c; Left = l; Right = r
Cover Science Photo Library (SPL)/Jeremy Bishop; Pages 5 Shutterstock/Vulkanette; 6 Corbis/Vince Streano;
7 Corbis/Gary Braasch; 10 Getty/Colin Anderson; 12–13 Corbis/C. Brad Lewis; 13 Corbis/Michelle Garrett;
15 & 16 Amy Nichole Harris; 17 Alamy/The Art Gallery; 18 Corbis/Paul Souders; 19c Shutterstock/David P.
Lewis; 19b Shutterstock/Andy Z.; 21 Getty/Mike Theiss; 22 SPL/Anakaopress/Look at Sciences;
23 SPL/Jeremy Bishop; 24–25 Shutterstock/zschnepf; 25 Shutterstock/nikolpetr;
26–27 Corbis/Bo Zaunders; 27 Corbis/Bob Grist; 28 NASA/JPL.

A volcano erupts!

Mount St. Helens is a volcano in the state of Washington. It erupted in 1850. Then it was quiet. Snow and ice covered its **peak**. Thick forests grew on the sides of the mountain. Deer, wildcats, and other animals lived there. It was a peaceful place for 130 years.

That all changed in 1980. Mount St. Helens suddenly erupted! There was a huge **blast**, and great clouds of smoke shot out of the peak. The snow and ice melted, and water ran down the mountain.

Red-hot fact!
Before it erupted in 1980, Mount St. Helens was 9,850 feet (3,000 meters) high.

After the eruption

The eruption changed Mount St. Helens.
Part of its peak blew away. A hole was
blasted in its side. All its snow and
ice melted.

Forests were destroyed and many animals were killed. Fifty-seven people died.

The forests are growing again. Animals and people have returned. But the volcano could erupt again.

Can you see how the eruption changed Mount St. Helens? Look back at the photo on page 6.

Red-hot fact!
Mount St. Helens is now 8,200 feet (2,500 meters) high.

What's inside?

The opening to a volcano is called a **crater**. The opening goes down to a deep, hot place inside Earth. It is so hot that rocks melt!

Hot, melted rock inside Earth is called **magma**. Sometimes magma rises up from inside Earth. It comes out through the crater. When magma comes out of a volcano, it is called **lava**.

Red-hot fact!
Every day about 20 volcanoes erupt on Earth.

The lava flows down the mountain.
It cools and hardens. It forms a layer
on the side of the mountain.

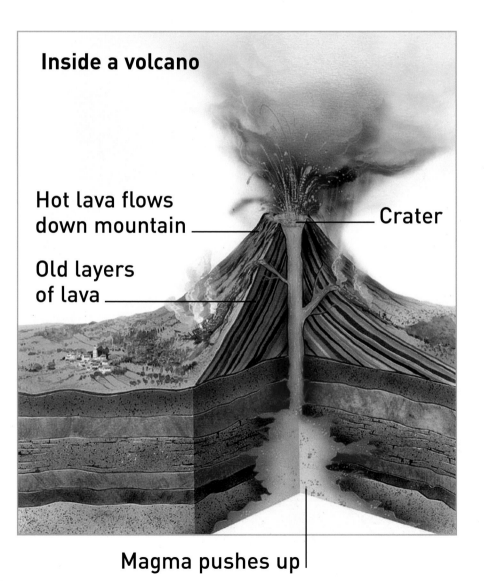

Inside a volcano

Hot lava flows
down mountain

Crater

Old layers
of lava

Magma pushes up

Run for your life!

Volcanic eruptions are not all the same. In some eruptions, lava **seeps** out slowly. People and animals have time to escape. But other eruptions happen fast and are very dangerous!

Hot rocks and lava can burn and crush people and animals. Burning lava can also

Red-hot fact!
Lava can move 30 miles (50 kilometers) an hour—*much* faster than a person can run.

destroy farms, villages, and roads. Ash coats everything in its path. And gases make the air hard to breathe.

This house in Sicily has been buried in lava.

An ancient eruption

About 2,000 years ago, a volcano in Italy suddenly erupted. It was called Mount Vesuvius. The volcano was near a town called Pompeii (say "Pom-PAY").

One afternoon, the townspeople heard a loud bang. They looked up and saw

a cloud of ash shoot
out of the top of
Mount Vesuvius.
Soon after, the town
was hit by falling rocks.

People ran out of their houses, but they
could not breathe in the clouds of gas
and ash. By evening, thousands had died.

The next day, more ash and lumps of lava
poured over the town. They hardened into
rock, and Pompeii was hidden.

Today
Mount
Vesuvius
overlooks
the ruins
of Pompeii.

Under the ash

Pompeii lay hidden for 1,500 years.
Then one day, people who were digging
a well came across some old ruins.
They were the ruins of Pompeii.

Soon teams of people came to dig. They
found old streets, shops, and fine houses.

These old streets were
dug out of the rock.

This wall painting shows a Roman baker with loaves of bread.

They found **bronze** statues and wonderful paintings. The digging went on. More than half the town has now been dug out of the rock. Today people from all over the world visit Pompeii to see what life was like in the past.

Red-hot fact!
More than two million people visit Pompeii every year.

Ready to erupt?

There are thousands of volcanoes on Earth. But they are not all ready to erupt.

Active volcano

An active volcano may erupt every day or rarely. One may be erupting right now!

This volcano in Iceland erupted in 2010.

Red-hot fact!
Earth has more than 1,500 active volcanoes.

Dormant volcano

A dormant volcano could have erupted hundreds of years ago. It has not erupted for a very long time. But it could wake up and erupt again.

Mount Callaghan is a dormant volcano in Canada.

Extinct volcano

An extinct volcano is very old and will never erupt again.

Diamond Head is an extinct volcano in Hawaii.

Volcanoes under the sea

There are even volcanoes under the sea! They erupt in the same way as volcanoes on land. Lava comes out of the crater. It cools and hardens as layers. The mountain grows bigger every time the volcano erupts. The tallest ones rise above the surface. They become islands!

The tallest mountain on Earth is an undersea volcano. Mauna Kea is 33,460 feet (10,200 meters) tall—that's 4,430 feet (1,350 meters) taller than Mount Everest!

Red-hot fact!
There are about 1,000 volcanoes under the sea.

Mauna Kea rises out of the sea.

One hot subject!

Some people study volcanoes and try to **predict** when they will erupt. These **experts** measure the size of a volcano to see if magma under the ground is making the mountain swell. They check to see if the ground is getting hotter.

Volcano experts work in dangerous places. They have to wear special heat-proof clothes. They crawl into craters to collect rock, ash, and gas. Their work is important and saves lives.

Visit a volcano

Many volcanoes are safe to visit. You can even walk to the top and look down into the crater. You may even smell the gases inside Earth. They smell like rotten cabbages and eggs!

Crater Lake in Oregon is on the site of an extinct volcano that last erupted 8,000 years ago. The deep lake is full of clear water. Many people go swimming and sailing there.

Walkers
explore
a volcano
in Japan.

Red-hot fact!
Crater Lake is 1,958
feet (597 meters)
deep. It is the
deepest lake in
the United States.

Crater Lake
is now a
national park.

The value of volcanoes

Volcanoes can be helpful to people.
Some farmers live near active volcanoes.
The ash is good for the soil. It helps
plants grow.

The water
in this lake
in Iceland is
heated by
volcanic rocks.

Volcanoes are useful in another way.
The rocks in the ground around them are
very hot. People use this heat to warm
their homes, schools, and swimming pools.
Heat from volcanoes is free and it never

runs out. In Iceland,
it is even used to
grow bananas.

Growing bananas
in Iceland

Volcanoes in space

There are volcanoes on some other planets and moons too.

Jupiter has a moon called Io. The dots all over Io's surface are very big, active volcanoes. A volcano is erupting next to the orange area in the photo below.

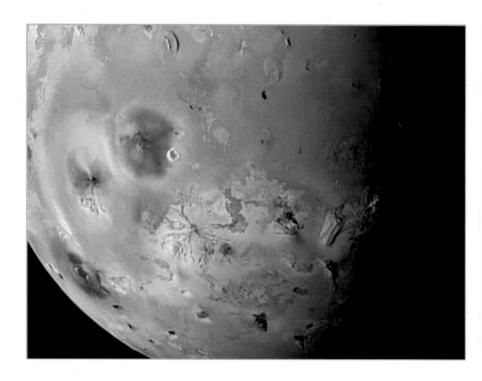

Olympus Mons is a volcano on Mars. It is 88,500 feet (27 kilometers) high—about three times higher than Mount Everest!

On Earth or in space, active volcanoes are powerful forces of nature!

Glossary

ash the soft, gray dust that is left after a volcano erupts

blast a big bang or explosion

bronze a red-brown metal

crater the bowl-like hole at the top of a volcano

erupt to throw out lava, ash, and gas

eruptions when volcanoes erupt

experts people who know a lot about something

gases very light, shapeless substances that you cannot see. Air is made of gases

lava the hot, melted rock that comes out of a volcano

magma the hot, melted rock inside
Earth

peak the pointed top of a mountain

predict to say what will happen in the
future

seeps flows slowly

Index